SHARING
OUR HOMELAND

PALESTINIAN AND JEWISH CHILDREN
AT SUMMER PEACE CAMP

BY TRISH MARX

PHOTOGRAPHS BY CINDY KARP

LEE & LOW BOOKS INC.
New York

ACKNOWLEDGMENTS

A great deal of cooperation and cross-cultural help was needed for this book to reach readers. Many thanks to the following people for their time and valuable input: Mohammad Darawshe, Co-Executive Director, The Abraham Fund Initiatives, Israel, and former Deputy Director General, Givat Haviva, Israel; Said Arda, head of the youth department, Menashe Regional Council, Israel, and his wife, Jutta; Samina Mahamed, librarian, Givat Haviva; the family of Yuval Oliel; the family of Alya Aduhadba; Saleem Yahea, translator; Rabbi Daniel Polish, spiritual director, Congregation Shir Chadash of the Hudson Valley, Lagrangeville, NY, and adjunct professor of world religions, Mount Saint Mary College, Newburgh, NY; Ami Nahshon, President and CEO, The Abraham Fund Initiatives, New York; Carrie Silberman, Rachel Henry, and Heather Paulson, librarians, New York Society Library; and Hanan Watson, Just Vision. A special thanks to Claudette and Issa Habesch, Patrick Marx, and all at Givat Haviva who so warmly welcomed us into the community. Finally, this list would not be complete without a thank-you to Louise May, our editor, for her vision and dedication to this book.

Engraving of Anata (Anathoth), Hill Country, Judea, on page 10 drawn by W. H. Bartlett, engraved by E. Brandard (ca. 1850). Used courtesy of Le Voyage en Papier–Marc Dechow.

Map on page 11 created by Paul Colin, Cezanne Studio, New York, NY.

LEE & LOW BOOKS Inc., 95 Madison Avenue, New York, NY 10016
leeandlow.com
Manufactured in China by Millenium International Limited, April 2010
Book design by Paul Colin, Cezanne Studio
Book production by The Kids at Our House
The text is set in Souvenir
10 9 8 7 6 5 4 3 2 1
First Edition
Library of Congress Cataloging-in-Publication Data
Marx, Trish.
Sharing our homeland : Palestinian and Jewish children at summer peace camp / by Trish Marx ; photographs by Cindy Karp. — 1st ed.
p. cm.
Summary: "Photo-essay focusing on two Israeli children, one Jewish and one Palestinian, who, in spite of their differences and
the longstanding conflicts in the region, learn to play, work, and share ideas together at Summer Peace Camp, a day camp located in Israel.
Includes glossary, map, and resources for readers"—Provided by publisher.
ISBN 978-1-58430-260-5 (hardcover : alk. paper)
1. Camps—Israel—Juvenile literature. 2. Jewish-Arab relations—Juvenile literature.
3. Judaism—Relations—Islam—Juvenile literature. 4. Islam—Relations—Judaism—Juvenile literature. I. Karp, Cindy, ill. II. Title.
GV195.I75M37 2010   915.69406'8—dc22   2009040311

FOR MOHAMMAD, CLAUDETTE,
AND IN MEMORY OF YEDIDA AND
JOHN —T.M.

FOR MY FATHER AND MOTHER,
WHO TAUGHT ME STRENGTH AND
TOLERANCE —C.K.

Summer is here, and Alya and Yuval are off to camp.
They will swim and play games, sing and make crafts,
go on field trips and spend a night sleeping in tents.
They will have fun with their friends and make new ones.
They will go home tired but excited for the next day at camp.
In these ways Alya and Yuval are like children
who go to camp anywhere.
But in other important ways they are different.
They are from two separate ethnic and religious groups
who share the same land
but who have been in conflict for the past one hundred years.
The country they live in is Israel.
Although their communities are close to each other,
Alya and Yuval have totally different lives.
They attend different schools, shop in different stores,
celebrate different holidays, and worship in different ways.
It is only at this camp that they will have the chance
to meet and come together—not as enemies,
but as campers,
as children,
and maybe, as friends.

Alya

Meiser is an Arab village of sixteen hundred people in north-central Israel. It sits on a rise of land, so when you see Meiser from a distance, the sun-washed stone houses built close together look like a pale golden blanket covering the hill. The landscape has looked like this for hundreds of years.

This is the village of Alya, an Israeli Palestinian girl. Alya and her family are Muslims, followers of Islam. They live in a large house with a porch, where they sit outside on hot summer nights.

Alya's parents are the center of the family. Her mother, Wedad, is a homemaker. Her father, Ahmed, is a businessman. Alya is the youngest child, which is why she is sometimes called "the last of the grapes." Two of her older sisters are married and have moved close to their husbands' families, a custom in their culture. A third older sister has finished high school and lives at home, helping their mother. Alya's older brother and his wife and baby live in an apartment built on top of Alya's house. Her brother's home is reached by wide, outdoor steps.

Living near one another and sharing food, wages, and household chores is a traditional way of life for many Palestinian families in the region. Alya can count more than two hundred relatives in her village.

YUVAL

A short distance from Meiser is Maor, a *moshav* where about five hundred people live. A moshav is a Jewish community made up of individually owned small farms.

Maor was started almost sixty years ago on a sunny stretch of land that needed only water to turn it into rich farmland. The land was irrigated and planted with vegetables and flowers. People living in the moshav share the costs of buying the equipment and supplies they need to farm. They also share the profits from the products they grow and sell. Each family lives in its own home, and family members may work on their farm or at other jobs in the moshav or outside the community. For security, a high fence with razor wire on top surrounds Maor. A sturdy, heavy gate guards the only road in and out.

Maor is home to Yuval, an Israeli Jewish boy, and his family. He lives with his mother, Aliza, who is a nurse; his father, Shalom, who is a carpenter; and his younger sister. His two older sisters are away for most of the year serving in the Israeli armed forces.

Both sets of Yuval's grandparents moved to Israel from Morocco in 1948, when Israel became independent. One grandmother still lives in the small town near Jerusalem where she settled so many years ago.

THE HOLY LAND

Even though Alya and Yuval live near each other, they could live their entire lives and not meet. In fact, they could spend their whole lives being afraid to meet, because the Palestinians and the Jews have fought for a long time over the land on which they live. Both groups claim it as their homeland, and their stories go back to ancient times.

Millions of people around the world believe the land known as Israel is their religion's Holy Land. It is where Judaism and Christianity began, and it is also sacred to Islam. Jews lived in the Holy Land in ancient times, but after they were conquered by the Babylonians in 586 B.C.E. and then by the Roman Empire in 70 C.E., many Jewish people fled to other parts of the world. In the seventh century C.E. the Arab ancestors of the Palestinians settled in the area. For the next several centuries there were periods of conflict and periods of relative peace among the peoples living in the Holy Land.

Beginning in 1517 the area was under Turkish rule for four hundred years. In 1917, during World War I, the British took control of the Holy Land, and called it Palestine. The British promised the Jewish people a homeland in Palestine and also promised to protect the rights of the Palestinians living there. Many Jews moved to the area and began work to create their own state. As more and more people arrived, tensions rose. Clashes among the Jews, Palestinians, and British erupted. Eventually, in 1937, the Palestinians called for their own independent nation.

In 1947 the United Nations recommended that Palestine be divided, with the idea of creating two separate states: one Palestinian and one Jewish. The Palestinians rejected this plan. They did not want to give up their land. The Jews accepted the plan and in 1948 established the independent nation of Israel. Several neighboring Arab nations, which supported the Palestinians, then went to war with Israel. Israel succeeded in defending itself and took control of more of Palestine. The rest was held by Egypt and Jordan. In 1967 war broke out between Israel and Egypt, Jordan, and Syria—a conflict known as the Six Day War. Israel won and expanded into the rest of Palestine.

The land then consisted of Israel and two areas controlled by Israel: the West Bank and the Gaza Strip. These areas, known as the Occupied Palestinian Territories, are where many Palestinians live today, while others live in Israel, outside the boundaries of the Territories, and are Israeli citizens.

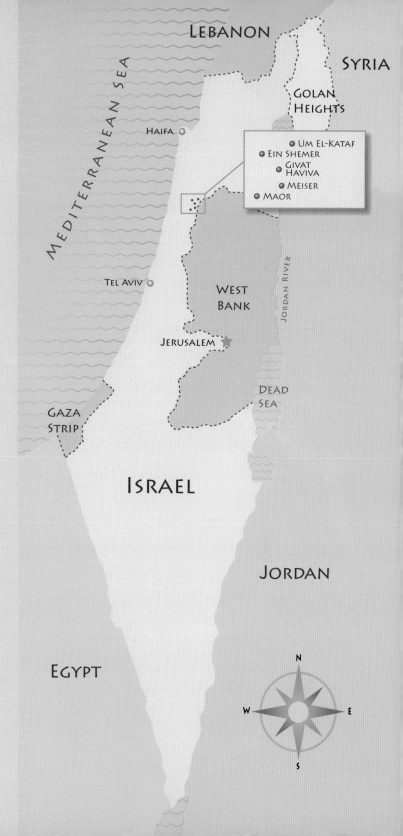

After the Six Day War, the United Nations called for Israel
to withdraw from the Territories and allow the creation of a
Palestinian state. This was not done. Over the years there
have been talks to try and find a peaceful resolution, but none
has been successful. Violence and conflict continue between
Israel and the Palestinians over land both feel belongs to them.
They have not yet been able to come to an agreement about
how to resolve their differences peacefully.

Alya and Yuval live in the midst of this ongoing conflict,
so when they learn that their parents are sending them to
day camp with both Palestinian and Jewish children, their
excitement is mixed with apprehension. Parents such as
Alya's and Yuval's know it is important for their children to
meet in a safe place and try to understand each other. But all
Alya and Yuval can think about is: What will children from the
"other side" be like? Will they have fun together? Could they
be friends?

Off to Camp

Early in the morning on the first day of camp, buses head out to pick up the campers. One bus picks up Alya in Meiser and another collects Yuval in Maor. Yuval is wearing shorts and a T-shirt. Alya is wearing long pants, a top, and a hijab, the head scarf worn by some Muslim girls and women.

When the buses arrive at camp, counselors walk the children to a shady pine grove. The camp is held for two weeks on the grounds of Givat Haviva, an educational organization that works toward Jewish-Arab peace. Alya reads the name of the camp in Arabic: Mukhayam Asalam. Yuval reads it in Hebrew: Kaytanat HaShalom. In English the name is Menashe Summer Peace Camp, but everybody—no matter what language he or she speaks—just calls it Peace Camp.

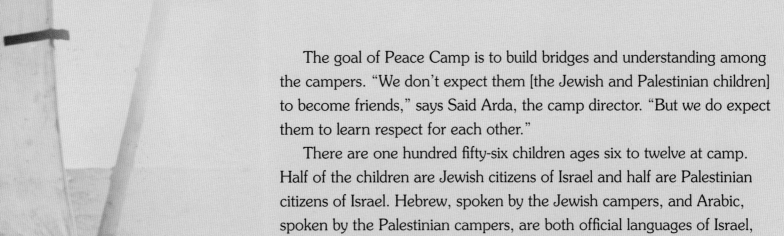

The goal of Peace Camp is to build bridges and understanding among the campers. "We don't expect them [the Jewish and Palestinian children] to become friends," says Said Arda, the camp director. "But we do expect them to learn respect for each other."

There are one hundred fifty-six children ages six to twelve at camp. Half of the children are Jewish citizens of Israel and half are Palestinian citizens of Israel. Hebrew, spoken by the Jewish campers, and Arabic, spoken by the Palestinian campers, are both official languages of Israel, and everything at camp is written in both languages. Still, communicating with one another is tough. The campers use sign language, nods, and some simple Hebrew and Arabic words they all know, along with smiles as they start feeling more comfortable.

The campers are divided into small groups with counselors who speak their language. Each group gathers inside its tent. For a few minutes the campground is quiet, but soon laughter and shouts erupt from each tent as the campers decide on a name. Alya's group chooses The Stars. Yuval's group is The Winners. The campers rush from their tents. It is time to decorate the tents with pictures and their group names.

There is a big pool on the grounds of Givat Haviva, and the campers cannot wait to jump in. Over the next few days, Peace Camp is like summer camp anywhere. The campers . . .

    play games in the pool,

        skim down a water slide,

            spend a day at the beach,

                create arts and crafts projects,

                  and try new things.

17

SPECIAL DAYS

When Said feels the campers are ready for some competition, he calls them together. "It's Olympics Day today," he announces.

The campers travel to a gently sloping hill in a park near the camp. Children line up behind their counselors. Sammy, the cook, microphone manager, and all-around everybody's friend, stops the Arabic music blasting from the tape player and gives a mighty blow on his whistle. Counselors jump aside, and the games begin.

One group of campers hops in and out of tires. Another pairs up for
wheelbarrow races. Inside a small gym, campers climb onto the rungs
on a wall of ladders. They hope to touch the top before Sammy blows
his whistle and shouts for them to run to the next activity. Every camper
wants to compete in all the games before it is time to stop.

On another day, Said looks serious. "We have some special visitors today," he says. A police car, an ambulance, and a bomb squad van are parked under the trees. Firefighters, medics, police officers, and border guards are waiting by the vehicles. Nearby is a table with gas masks, sirens, helmets, guns, and bulletproof vests. Because of the conflict in their country, all the children are familiar with these items. The visitors are here to show how some of the equipment is used.

"Who wants to volunteer for an emergency rescue?" asks a medic. Several children raise their hands. The campers watch as a neck brace is snapped onto a boy, and he is carefully placed on a stretcher. Other children then help load the stretcher into the ambulance.

Next a police officer shows the campers gear that is used when a bomb is suspected or found. A remote-controlled robot rolls up, and the officer moves the robot's arms to show how it can safely pick up and remove an object that might be a bomb. The robot is controlled from a distance so no one gets hurt if there is an explosion. In some cases an officer has to get close to a suspicious object to dispose of it. He or she then puts on a heavy protective suit. "It is big and bulky and hot inside," says the officer. "But it keeps me safe if I have to handle a bomb."

Shortly before camp started, a bomb went off on a crowded shopping street in a town not far from Givat Haviva, killing several people. The children are aware of this incident, but Said does not talk about the bomb, who planted it, or why. Instead he tries to reassure the campers, telling them that people such as their visitors work hard every day to keep all the citizens of Israel safe.

The campers have lived with the possibility of violence their entire lives. When Alya was younger, a gunman from the West Bank broke into homes in a Jewish settlement near Meiser and killed several people. The government built a security fence around the settlement, and the people of both communities held meetings to talk about their fears. Yuval had violence come even closer. One night a terrorist from the West Bank broke into Maor and held two people hostage until the police came. For a long time afterward Yuval was afraid there would be another confrontation near his home.

In part because of incidents such as these, in 2002 the Israeli government began building a tall barrier around most of the West Bank. The barrier, which in places is 26 feet (8 meters) high, has helped reduce the number of bombings and other terrorist attacks. But it has also divided communities and kept people from getting to and from work freely and visiting relatives and friends on the other side of the barrier from where they live.

A few days later, the campers are off on a field trip. As the buses bounce along the road, the children sing loudly—first Jewish songs, then Arabic songs, and finally popular Western songs.

The first stop is kibbutz Ein Shemer. A kibbutz is a communal settlement where all property and the responsibilities for daily life are shared by everyone living there. Ein Shemer looks very much like it did in 1927, when it was settled by Jews from Poland. Most of the Palestinian campers have never been to a kibbutz, so this visit is a new experience for them.

In the museum on the kibbutz grounds, the children find figures of a Jewish settler and an Arab, both dressed in clothes from the 1920s. The guide explains that many of the settlers were from cities and did not know how to farm. The Arabs living nearby helped the Jewish settlers learn how plow the land and grow crops. In return, the Jews invited their neighbors to holiday celebrations and shared their native songs and stories.

Next the campers enter the baking house, with its long wooden tables and ovens built into the walls. The children are going to make their own loaves of challah, a braided bread eaten by Jews on their Sabbath. Alya is excited. She helps her mother with the cooking and baking at home, and even though she has not made challah before, she knows what to do. Yuval has eaten lots of challah, but he has never made bread. He looks at his ball of dough. It has to be kneaded, divided and formed into strips, and finally braided. Alya laughs and shows Yuval how to roll the dough and weave the strips into a braid.

The baking bread smells so good! When the loaves are done, they come out of the oven golden brown. Each child looks for his or her loaf. Yuval finds his: a tiny loaf that starts off lopsided, then is smoothly braided. He tears off a piece of the warm bread and gives it to Alya.

The second stop is the Arab village Um El-Kataf, high in the hills. This visit is something new for many of the Jewish children, who have probably never been to an Arab village.

The campers crowd onto the stone patio of a small house surrounded by olive trees swaying in the breeze. The children are here to make another kind of bread: the round flatbread called *taboon* that is commonly eaten in the region. Um Jehad, the woman who has opened her home to the campers, gives each child a small ball of dough. Using wooden rolling pins, the children flatten their dough balls into circles. After placing their dough on a large tray, the campers follow Um Jehad as she carries the tray on her head to a round, low structure. Inside, on the ground, is a traditional taboon oven: a metal plate covered with smooth stones and heated underneath by hot coals. She places a few circles of dough on the hot stones and puts the oven's cone-shaped lid in place.

"Now it's time for tea," Um Jehad says. The campers walk a short distance to the room where guests are entertained. The thick stone walls keep the room cool inside. As the campers sit on the colorful rugs covering the floor and drink mint tea, a drummer joins them and begins beating out the rhythms of the coffee men. Years ago, peddlers called coffee men would walk through the surrounding villages drumming on wooden jugs and selling coffee.

When all the taboon is ready, the campers walk back to the patio. Eagerly they munch their bread, dipping it in olive oil and then in *zaatar*, a popular mixture of dried herbs.

The last visit of the day is to the museum in Um El-Kataf. The items on display include looms, pots, baskets, and tools of all sorts. They were used by villagers for farming and home life until the middle of the twentieth century. The pots, made from clay found in the area, once held olive oil or water. The children try to imagine people carrying around big, heavy pots of oil and water instead of the smaller bottles their families use today.

At Home with Alya

After camp on Friday, Alya and her mother go to the mosque in Meiser to pray. Friday is a special day of prayer for Muslims. In the mosque, men and women pray in separate rooms. Alya kneels next to her mother, then bends forward and touches her forehead to the carpet. They face toward Mecca, the city where the *ka'bah* is located. The ka'bah is the building in which the sacred black stone of Islam is found. On other days Alya usually prays at home.

Alya wears a hijab both outside and inside her home. "I wanted to be a religious person since I was a very little girl," she says. Wearing a hijab is a way for Alya to express her connection to her religion.

"This was special for her," says Alya's mother. "She had freedom to choose. Two of her sisters chose not to wear a hijab."

On Saturday, when camp is closed, Alya helps her mother and sisters in the kitchen. They cut tomatoes, stir beef and vegetable stew, and cook rice. Alya puts olives and pickles into small dishes to place around the table so everyone will have a dish within easy reach. The dining room is where Alya and her sister sleep. At mealtimes, their low beds are pushed aside and the table is set. When the family sits down to the midday meal, the table is covered with some of Alya's favorite foods.

Alya would like to be a teacher when she grows up. She would also like to be a counselor at Peace Camp. "That would be an important thing to do," Alya says. "We live together in the same country, but we don't know each other. One day there will be a peace between the Palestinians and the Jews, and camp will help us learn to live together."

At Home with Yuval

Yuval hops off the bus from camp on Friday afternoon. He gives his mother a hug and says hi to his little sister. When Yuval's father gets home, he reads the newspaper with the children. They talk about local news, sports, and what is happening around the world.

The Jewish Sabbath begins on Friday at sunset. With the family gathered at the table, Yuval's mother lights two candles just before the sun sets to welcome the Sabbath. Next Yuval's father says the blessing over the wine, and then he blesses the children. Finally everyone joins in saying the blessing over the bread and eats a small piece of challah dipped in salt.

Then it is time for dinner. Yuval especially likes the Friday night meal his family always prepares: tomato and cucumber salads, potatoes, and chicken baked with apricots. For dessert they have baklava, a sweet pastry made with nuts and honey.

Yuval's older sisters, Malki and Hadar, are home on leave from serving in the Israeli armed forces. Malki is in the navy, and Hadar is in the army. At age eighteen, Jewish boys and girls are required to serve in the military. Boys serve for three years, and girls serve for two years. Boys and girls who are excused for religious or medical reasons may perform their national service in nonmilitary jobs.

Hadar joined the army because she wants to serve her country. "Growing up, I saw a lot of news on the TV and in the newspapers, and I always knew I wanted to do something . . . to give back to the country, to those who get wounded or hurt or somehow die."

"Yuval sees what his sisters are doing," says his mother. "He is less afraid now of violence. He is more worried about the camp sleepover. He wants to sleep next to the counselor!"

THE SLEEPOVER

The sleepover! This is what the campers have been looking forward to since the first day of camp two weeks ago. It is also the first time many of the children will be sleeping away from home.

Campers arrive with their families, who have been invited for the evening's activities. The children carry pillows and blankets, backpacks and stuffed animals. Squeals of laughter ring through the pine grove as the campers stake out places to sleep in their tents.

When the sun starts to set, the shadows grow longer. The dark edges of the pine grove begin to look a little scary.

"We need to make torches," say the counselors. They roll black paper into cones and give one to each child to fill with a cushion of pine needles. Each camper then inserts a small flashlight into the center of the cushion, and a counselor staples yellow plastic over the open end of the cone. Armed with light, the children race through the camp until Sammy rings the dinner bell.

Hungry campers and their families dish up salads and French fries, grilled hamburgers and lamb sausages. The DJ booms music through the grounds as parents and children dig into their food. Some campers get up and dance, alone or with friends, and soon a line of children is snaking through the crowd.

After dinner Said calls everyone to the talent show. The counselors sing funny songs and read poems they have written about the past two weeks at camp. Some songs and poems are in Hebrew and some are in Arabic, but everyone laughs at seeing the counselors act so silly.

As darkness falls, a group of jugglers performs. The jugglers toss balls over their heads, four and five at a time, catching and tossing them again and again. Next they throw lit torches high in the air, faster and faster. The crowd gasps as the jugglers seem to disappear inside circles of flame. Then, to everyone's amazement, the jugglers finish by tossing knives, the blades flashing brightly in the night.

Finally the families say their good-byes. A few parents are
spending the night to help watch over the children. The campers
settle down for the last fun activity of the evening: the movie
Hercules. The film shows how a baby born to a Greek god loses
his immortality and has to earn it back by performing amazing feats
of courage. Courage and fun are part of what the campers have
experienced at Peace Camp too.

By the time the campers get up the next morning, the sun has dried the mist off the grass and all the scary corners in the pine grove have disappeared. Everything looks friendly and peaceful.

A counselor sings softly while tapping his drum. After breakfast the children pack their gear and roll up their tents. Then they head off to the swimming pool to play in the water one last time. A camper walks by wearing a T-shirt that reads: THE UNSPOKEN WORD NEVER DOES HARM. The counselors hope the children are a little closer to understanding this statement than they were before they came to camp.

Soon lunch arrives. Pizza! The campers gobble their slices, then top off their meal with "grandmother's hair," fine-spun cotton candy rolled onto paper cones.

After lunch everyone gathers for a performance by the Capoeira Dancers. Capoeira was created hundreds of years ago by African slaves in Brazil. It was a way for the slaves to trick their owners into thinking they were dancing when they were actually practicing their traditional fighting skills. Today capoeira is enjoyed as a game, an acrobatic dance, and a martial art.

Said chose the Capoeira Dancers for the campers' last day because, along with being exciting to watch, capoeira stresses mutual respect, equality, and shared experiences. These are the same things Said had asked the children to think about whenever disagreements arose or campers were upset with each other.

Saying Good-Bye

It is the end of the camp session. The days have passed in a hurry. Alya and Yuval gather their friends around them. They raise their hands in the peace sign, then hug their counselors and wave good-bye.

Some children will come back to camp next year. Others will go to different camps or summer activities. But all the campers have been changed in some small way by their two weeks at Peace Camp. Maybe a child learned to swim across the pool by himself or herself. Maybe a child learned how to say a few new words in another language. And maybe some children, like Alya and Yuval, made a new friend, someone from the "other side."

These may seem like small changes, but they are important to these children, who might have been afraid to meet before coming to camp. In a country filled with tension and conflict, the campers have learned to take the first steps toward sharing their ancient homeland. And it happens every year, year after year, at Peace Camp.

Further Reading

Carmi, Daniella. *Samir and Yonatan*. New York: Scholastic/Blue Sky, 2002.

Ellis, Deborah. *Three Wishes: Palestinian and Israeli Children Speak*. Toronto: Groundwood, 2004.

Frank, Mitch. *Understanding the Holy Land: Answering Questions About the Israeli Palestinian Conflict*. New York: Viking, 2005.

Gunderson, Cory. *The Israeli-Palestinian Conflict*. Edina, MN: ABDO, 2004.

Koplewicz, Harold S., Gail C. Furman, and Robin F. Goodman. *Turbulent Times/Prophetic Dreams: Art from Israeli and Palestinian Children*. Englewood, NJ: Pitspopany Press, 2000.

Rifa'i, Amal, and Odelia Ainbinder, with Sylke Tempel. *We Just Want to Live Here: A Palestinian Teenager, an Israeli Teenager— an Unlikely Friendship*. New York: St. Martin's Griffin, 2003.

Tolan, Sandy. *The Lemon Tree: An Arab, a Jew, and the Heart of the Middle East*. New York: Bloomsbury, 2007.

Wallach, John, with Michael Wallach. *The Enemy Has a Face: The Seeds of Peace Experience*. Washington, DC: United States Institute of Peace Press, 2000.

Web Sites of Interest

Givat Haviva is an educational organization that works to further social justice and Jewish-Arab peace in Israel and neighboring Arab countries. www.givathaviva.org

Hand in Hand Center for Jewish-Arab Education develops bilingual, multicultural schools aimed at building peace between Jews and Arabs in Israel. www.handinhand12.org

Just Vision researches and documents Palestinian and Israeli nonviolent civilian efforts to resolve the conflict in the region. www.justvision.org

Knowledge is the Beginning is a film chronicling the story of the West-Eastern Divan Orchestra, where young Arabs and Jews perform and live side by side. www.knowledge-is-the-beginning.com

Oasis of Peace is a village of Jewish and Palestinian Israelis engaged in educational work for peace, equality, and understanding. www.nswas.org

Seeds of Peace brings together youth from areas of conflict to discuss how to advance reconciliation and coexistence. www.seedsofpeace.org

The Abraham Fund Initiatives is an organization that works to advance coexistence, equality, and cooperation among Jewish and Arab citizens in Israel. www.abrahamfund.org

Author's Note

My first visit to Israel was years ago, in December. The wind whipped me through the narrow, cobbled streets of the Old City of Jerusalem. Icy rain fell, but I walked for hours each day. With each step I took, I felt the jolt of thousands of years of history. Israel was so different from what I had imagined. A very small country, it kept getting bigger and bigger as the layers of time unfolded.

I went back to Israel several times, and each time I met new people and heard their stories. Everyone had a different background and a different perspective. I began to understand what was behind the years of conflict between the Palestinian and Jewish people living there. I also saw many examples of Palestinians and Jews trying to live together in peace and with respect for one another.

Yedida Lalav, a Jewish woman born in Palestine in 1911, told me about her Palestinian neighbors lighting her family's cooking fire on the Sabbath. In turn, Yedida's family brought food to her Palestinian neighbors during times of sickness. Mohammad Darawshe, a Palestinian citizen of Israel from Iksal, a small village near Nazareth, attended both Arab and Jewish schools, and his work for peaceful coexistence between Palestinians and Jews in Israel has earned him several international awards. It was Mohammad who told me about Givat Haviva's Menashe Summer Peace Camp. "You should see it," he said. Go to camp? I could hardly wait! My best summers growing up were spent at Camp Olson in northern Minnesota. Photographer Cindy Karp and I were off to camp!

I brought my tape recorder, notebooks, a slew of pens, and dozens of tapes. Cindy brought her cameras and a mind-boggling array of equipment for the several thousand pictures she would take while we were at camp. Each day we spread out, checking our lists for the photos and interviews we needed in order to tell the story of the camp experience.

We stayed at a peaceful kibbutz, our rooms under an ancient, towering tree. One evening we were invited to Alya's home for sweet tea, orange slices, and a viewing of wedding videos. Another evening we visited a small café owned by Yuval's family and talked for hours to one of his sisters about her life and military service. Said Arda took us to an Arab town close to Givat Haviva to see the tall, concrete barrier that surrounds much of the West Bank. We put on hijabs and entered the mosque in Meiser.

Throughout our stay in Israel, Cindy and I knew we were documenting just one story about a very complex part of the world where there are many compelling stories. What took place at Peace Camp was important, however, because it offered a message of peace and hope not often heard from this region. The premise of the story sounds pretty normal: two kids go to summer camp. But it was a camp that can change perspectives, futures, and perhaps the future of a country.

Trish Marx, 2010

Pronunciation Guide and Glossary

Because some sounds in Hebrew and Arabic have no exact equivalents in English, the pronunciations for Hebrew and Arabic words and names are approximate. The spellings of these words and names in English may also vary.

Arab (A-ruhb): member of one of the Arabic-speaking peoples living in the Middle East and northern Africa

Arabic (A-ruh-bik): language spoken by many people in the Middle East and northern Africa; having to do with Arabia, the Arabs, their religion, or their culture

Babylonian (ba-buh-LOH-nee-uhn): person who lived in Babylonia, an ancient empire in southwestern Asia

baklava (BAH-kluh-vah *or* bah-kluh-VAH): dessert made of layers of thin pastry, nuts, and honey

B.C.E.: abbreviation for Before Common Era; indicates a date before year 1 in the Western calendar

capoeira (kah-poo-WAY-rah): Brazilian game, dance, and martial art

C.E.: abbreviation for Common Era; indicates a date from year 1 or later in the Western calendar

challah (hAH-luh): rich bread containing eggs that is usually braided before baking; traditionally eaten by Jews on the Sabbath and holidays

Christian (KRIS-chuhn): person who practices the religion of Christianity

Christianity (kris-chee-AN-uh-tee): religion of Christians, based on the life and teachings of Jesus

Ein Shemer (ayn SHEH-mehr): kibbutz settled by Polish Jews in 1927

ethnic group (ETH-nik groop): people who share a common origin or heritage based on race, culture, religion, nationality, and/or language

Gaza Strip (GAH-zuh strip): small area of land on the southeast coast of the Mediterranean Sea; part of the Occupied Palestinian Territories

Givat Haviva (geev-AHT hah-VEE-vah): international educational organization, founded in 1949, that works for social justice and the advancement of Jewish-Arab peace in Israel and neighboring Arab countries

Hebrew (HEE-broo): language spoken by Jewish people in Israel and other areas of the world

hijab (hee-JAB): head scarf worn by a Muslim girl or woman that covers her hair and neck

Holy Land (HOH-lee land): area in the Middle East on the east coast of the Mediterranean Sea that Jews, Muslims, and Christians believe is sacred

immortality (i-mor-TA-luh-tee): endless life

irrigate (IHR-uh-gate): to supply land with water by artificial means, such as channels or pipes

Islam (iss-LAHM): religion of Muslims, based on the teachings of Allah (God) as revealed to the prophet Muhammad; Arabic word meaning "submission"

Israel (IZ-ree-uhl): country in the Middle East bordering the Mediterranean Sea; declared a Jewish state in 1948

Israeli (iz-RAY-lee): person born or living in Israel; of or having to do with Israel or its people

Jerusalem (jeh-ROO-suh-luhm): capital of Israel; ancient holy city for Jews, Christians, and Muslims

Jew (joo): person who practices the religion of Judaism

Jewish (JOO-ish): having to do with Jews, their religion, or their culture

Judaism (JOO-dee-iz-uhm *or* JOO-dey-iz-uhm): religion of Jews, based on the belief in one God and the teachings of the Old Testament

ka'bah (KAH-bah): holy building in Mecca in which the sacred black stone of Islam is located

Kaytanat HaShalom (kai-tah-NAHT hah-shah-LOME): Hebrew for Peace Camp

kibbutz (ki-BUHTS): communal Israeli settlement, traditionally a farm, based on equality, joint ownership of property, and shared responsibilities

Maor (mah-OHR): moshav in north-central Israel

Mecca (MEH-kuh): city in Saudi Arabia; spiritual center of Islam

medic (MEH-dik): person trained to give medical help in an emergency

Meiser (MAY-sahr): Arab village in north-central Israel

Menashe (meh-nah-SHEH): region in Israel consisting of twenty Jewish and Arab communities; Maor, Meiser, Ein Shemer, and Um El-Kataf are all in the Menashe region

moshav (moh-SHAHV): cooperative Israeli community consisting of small, individually owned farms that rely on shared purchasing and selling of products

mosque (mosk): Muslim place of worship

Mukhayam Asalam (moo-hah-YAM ah-sah-LAM): Arabic for Peace Camp

Muslim (MUHZ-luhm *or* MUSS-lim): person who follows the religion of Islam

Occupied Palestinian Territories (OK-yuh-pyed pah-luh-STIN-ee-uhn TER-uh-tor-eez): West Bank and Gaza Strip; also referred to as "disputed territories"

Palestine (PAH-luh-stine): name used historically for the Holy Land

Palestinian (pah-luh-STIN-ee-uhn): person born or living in Palestine

Roman Empire (ROH-muhn EM-pire): lands and people who were ruled by ancient Rome; at its peak the Roman Empire controlled areas in Europe, Africa, and Asia

Sabbath (SA-buhth): day of the week set aside for rest and worship in some religions; observed by Jews from sundown Friday to sundown Saturday and by most Christians on Sunday

taboon (tah-BOON): Middle Eastern flatbread baked in a taboon oven

taboon oven (tah-BOON UH-vehn): traditional outdoor oven with a fire built under a metal plate on which smooth rocks are placed

terrorist (TER-er-ist): person who uses violence and threats to frighten others

Um El-Kataf (oom el-kah-TAF): Arab village in north-central Israel

West Bank (west bangk): region on the west bank of the Jordan River; part of the Occupied Palestinian Territories

zaatar (ZAH-tahr): blend of herbs and seasonings used in Middle Eastern cooking; usually includes thyme, sesame seeds, sumac, and salt

NAMES OF PEOPLE

Ahmed (AH-mad)

Aliza (ah-LEE-zuh)

Alya (AL-yah)

Hadar (hah-DAHR)

Malki (MAL-key)

Said Arda (sah-EED AR-dah)

Shalom (shah-LOME)

Um Jehad (oom jeh-HAD)

Wedad (wee-DAD)

Yuval (yoo-VAHL)

AUTHOR'S SOURCES

This story is a depiction of actual events that took place in and around Israel's Menashe Summer Peace Camp in 2005. Some of the research was conducted while the author was in Israel and encompasses her primary experiences and observations, including conversations and discussions with campers, their families, and local officials, guides, and organizations.

Collins, Larry, and Dominique Lapierre. *O Jerusalem!* New York: Simon & Schuster, 2007.

Frank, Mitch. *Understanding the Holy Land: Answering Questions About the Israeli-Palestinian Conflict.* New York: Viking, 2005.

Friedman, Thomas L. *From Beirut to Jerusalem.* New York: Farrar, Straus & Giroux, 1989.

Gardner, Joseph L. ed. *Atlas of the Bible: An Illustrated Guide to the Holy Land.* Pleasantville, NY: Reader's Digest, 1981.

Miller, Aaron David. *The Too Much Promised Land: America's Elusive Search for Arab Israeli Peace.* New York: Bantam, 2008.

Said, Edward W. *The Question of Palestine.* New York: Vintage, 1992.

Sakakini, Hala. *Jerusalem and I: A Personal Record.* Jerusalem: Hala Sakakini, 1987.

Shipler, David K. *Arab and Jew: Wounded Spirits in the Promised Land.* New York: Times Books, 1986; updated ed.: Penguin, 2001.

Eshchar, Yochanan (Co-Principal of Wadi Ara Hand-in-Hand School, Kfar Kara, Israel). Interview, July 2005.

Interviews with Jewish and Palestinian families and counselors connected with Givat Haviva and Menashe Summer Peace Camp.

Numerous history texts, Web sites, magazine and newspaper articles, and other reference materials, read since the late 1980s, for historical and current information.